Mediterranean Diet for Beginners

55+ Easy Healthy Recipes for Natural Weight Loss

Contents

Introduction 6

  What is the Mediterranean Diet? 6

  Benefits of the Mediterranean Diet....................................8

  Mediterranean Diet Pyramid 10

  What to Eat... 11

  What to Avoid 12

How to the Make Mediterranean Diet Work for You...................**13**

  Top Hints of Success.. 13

Mediterranean Diet Recipes **17**

  Breakfast Recipes 17

    Yogurt Pancakes.. 18

    Eggs in Tomato Sauce... 20

    Date Smoothie... 22

    Veggie Omelet... 23

    Veggie Muffins 25

  Soup Recipes... 27

    Mixed Veggie Soup... 28

    Lentil & Spinach Soup 30

    Chicken & Pasta Soup.. 32

    Lamb, Lentils & Chickpeas Soup 34

    Tomato Soup.. 36

  Salad Recipes... 37

    Watermelon Salad 38

    Fresh Veggie Salad.. 39

    Chickpeas Salad 40

Chicken Salad 42

Tuna Salad 43

Fish & Seafood Recipes 45

Salmon with Capers 46

Tilapia in Herb Sauce 47

Salmon with Avocado Cream 48

Grilled Salmon 50

Tilapia with Capers 52

Almond Crusted Tilapia 54

Grilled Prawns 55

Halibut with Olives & Tomatoes 56

Cod in Tomato Sauce 58

Tuna with Olives Sauce 60

Mussels in Wine Sauce 62

Octopus in Honey Sauce 64

Seafood Paella 66

Seafood Stew 68

Garlicky Shrimp 70

Meat & Poultry Recipes 71

Spiced Lamb Chops 72

Leg of Lamb with Potatoes 74

Lamb Koftas with Yogurt Sauce 76

Beef Stew 78

Beef & Olives Bake 80

Chicken with Caper Sauce 82

Chicken Casserole 84

Chicken & Veggie Kabobs 86

Roasted Chicken.. 88

Lemony Chicken Breast.. 90

Pizza & Pasta Recipes.. 91

Veggie Pizza.. 92

Shrimp Pizza... 94

Pasta with Tomatoes 95

Pasta with Veggies 96

Pasta with Shrimp & Spinach.. 98

Vegetarian Recipes 99

Roasted Carrots.. 100

Chickpeas Hummus.. 101

Quinoa & Zucchini Fritters... 102

Chickpeas Stew... 104

Stuffed Tomatoes.. 106

Dessert Recipes 107

Roasted Pears.. 108

Chocolate Mousse... 110

Frozen Strawberry Yogurt.. 111

Tahini Cookies.. 112

Baklava... 114

Introduction

What is the Mediterranean Diet?

The Mediterranean diet is based upon the culture and cuisines of the Mediterranean region. Several medical and scientific studies have proved that the Mediterranean diet is very healthy and is a perfect diet plan for circumventing numerous chronic diseases like cardiac complications and cancer, in addition to improving life expectancy.

Medical researchers had started drawing connections between diet and cardiac complications in the 1950s. Dr. Ancel Keys studied several diets in accordance with the principles of epidemiology, known as the *Seven Countries Study,* which has been declared the most authentic epidemiological study ever conducted. The study was performed over a decade, involving around 13,000 male individuals from the US, Serbia, Japan, Finland, Croatia, and the Netherlands. The study was concluded on the fact that the people from the Mediterranean region had a lower risk of acquiring a chronic heart disease and enjoyed more healthy lifestyles as compared to the rest of the globe. The study also argued that the mortality rate of the Mediterranean region was low compared to the rest of the world.

New scientific research has further backed the work of Dr. Ancel Keys about the healthy lifestyle of the Mediterranean people. A report issued in 1990 by the

WHO (World Health Organization) argued that European Mediterranean countries like Italy, Greece, Spain, and France have a higher life expectancy and lower risk of heart complications and cancer from the rest of Europe. The analysis proved life-changing as these countries have high smoking populations and do not have any appropriately conducted exercise programs like American society. The factor of genetic variations has been rejected by scientists because those Mediterranean people who travel to other countries and get a break from the Mediterranean diet start losing the health benefits the diet offered. All these studies consider the fact that both diet and lifestyle are critically important factors.

The study also showed that the Mediterranean diet has 40 percent of its calories derived from high fat, making it very different in its fat intake from the rest of the diets. Mediterranean cuisine involves lower content of saturated fats and higher content of unsaturated fats, like olive oil. Saturated fats are present mainly in meat and dairy products, apart from their slight presence in a few nuts, certain vegetable oils, and avocados. Saturated fats are utilized by the body to make cholesterol and are strongly linked to cardiovascular issues.

The Mediterranean diet came into the limelight when Dr. Walter Willet, the head of the Nutrition Department of Harvard University, recommended it to various people. Low-fat oriented diets were already being recommended for heart issues. Mediterranean groups involved in his studies had a high-fat-oriented diet possessing their main fat content from olive oil. His studies argued that the risk of heart-related complications and diseases can be reduced by enhancing the intake of a type of dietary fat. This disagreement of Dr. Walter was entirely opposite to the generally applied nutritional recommendations and preferences of eradicating all types of fat content from diet plans to evade heart-related problems. Studies have concluded that unsaturated fats have been credited with a high amount of good cholesterol, known as HDL cholesterol. The reason for HDL cholesterol being ascribed as a friend for the body is due to the protection it provides to the body from cardiovascular complications. Dr. Willet also linked meat intake with cardiovascular diseases and cancer.

Benefits of the Mediterranean Diet

The Mediterranean diet has numerous health benefits for its followers if it is consistently followed. Some of the vital ones are as follows:

Lower Risk of Cardiovascular Complications

The Mediterranean diet has a strong constructive effect on heart-related risk factors like high BP, triglycerides, and cholesterol, due to which it minimizes the risk of attaining cardiovascular diseases, like myocardial infarction (commonly known as a heart attack), strokes, and coronary heart diseases.

Bone Strengthening

Olive oil is abundantly used in the Mediterranean diet due to its ability of increasing and preserving bone density by incrementing the maturity and proliferation of the bone cells. The Mediterranean diet patterns are also ascribed with preventing osteoporosis.

Memory Preservation

The Mediterranean diet is proved to be highly beneficial in preventing cognitive declines and preserving your memory. The reason is that the Mediterranean diet is high in its healthy fat content, which is super beneficial in avoiding the risk of cognitive decline and dementia, as well as stimulating the human brain. A study consistently claims that the risk of cognitive declines is reduced by around 40 percent by following the Mediterranean diet.

Cancer Preservation

The Mediterranean diet has been credited with anticancer properties. Research shows a 13 percent reduced risk of terminal cancer in those who follow the Mediterranean diet as compared to the non-followers. The various cancers that can be prevented by following the Mediterranean diet include liver cancer, neck cancer, breast cancer, head cancer, prostate cancer, gastric cancer, and colorectal cancer.

Anti-Depression

The Mediterranean diet is also popular for possessing anti-depressant characteristics. A study depicted that those who follow the Mediterranean diet plan has approximately 98.6 percent reduced risk of depression than the non-followers.

Blood Sugar Controlling

The Mediterranean diet has been proven to control body blood sugar levels and diabetes. It is also known to reverse type 2 diabetes and improve heart-related risks and blood sugar control.

Mediterranean Diet Pyramid

Dr. Willet and the WHO joined hands with various other researchers in 1994 and built the Mediterranean Food Pyramid. The Mediterranean Food Pyramid includes food from several categories and their intake amount per day in order to follow the Mediterranean diet plan perfectly. These researchers claim that their food groups are far more valuable in health status as compared to the food groups designed by the USDA (United States Department of Agriculture). The USDA has listed a higher content of daily dairy and meat servings. The Mediterranean diet specialists claim that these recommendations have nothing to do with dietary science at all and are politically motivated.

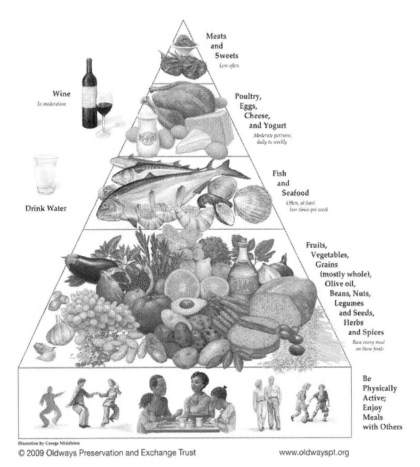

What to Eat

The Mediterranean diet has a wide variety of delicious food options for its followers. As there is certainly a variation between the counties, the exact foods for the diet are a bit controversial. The foods preferred to be consumed for following the Mediterranean **diet perfectly include:**

- Seeds and nuts like macadamia nuts, cashews, pumpkin seeds, almonds, walnuts, hazelnuts, sunflower seeds, etc.
- Dairy products like Greek yogurt, cheese, yogurt, etc.
- Seafood and fish like tuna, trout, shrimp, clams, crabs, sardines, mussels, salmon, etc.
- Veggies like, kale, carrots, broccoli, tomatoes, cauliflower, Brussels sprouts, spinach, cucumbers, etc.
- Spices and Herbs like basil, rosemary, nutmeg, pepper, mint, garlic, sage, cinnamon, etc.
- Fruits like oranges, strawberries, figs, peaches, melons, pears, apples, dates, bananas, grapes, etc.
- Eggs like quail eggs, duck eggs, and chicken eggs, etc.
- Whole grains like rye, corn, barley, wheat oats, whole wheat, pasta and bread (whole grain), brown rice, etc.
- Legumes like lentils, chickpeas, beans, peas, peanuts, etc.
- Poultry like turkey, chicken, duck, etc.
- Tubers like yams, sweet potatoes, turnips, potatoes, etc.
- Healthy fats like avocado oil, olive oil, olives, and avocados, etc.
- The preferred beverage for the Mediterranean diet is water. You can also drink coffee and tea, but it is preferable to avoid sugar-sweetened beverages, various fruit juices, and high-sugar drinks. You can also have approximately one to two glasses of wine daily. But wine should be avoided if you have any complications related to its intake.

While following the Mediterranean diet, certain important factors regarding **food must be kept in mind**:

- Eat dairy products and poultry moderately.
- Eat red meat rarely.
- Eat the rest of the foods in abundance.

What to Avoid

As stated earlier, the Mediterranean diet offers vast, delicious food options for its followers, but there are certain limitations associated with it. Foods that are preferred to be avoided for following the Mediterranean diet:

- Trans Fats containing foods like margarine and other processed foods.
- Processed meats like hot dogs, processed sausages, etc.
- Added sugars like soda, ice cream, soda, table sugar, and various other same products, etc.
- Highly processed foods i.e. anything labeled "low-fat" or "diet," which indicates that they have been manufactured in a factory.
- Refined oils like cottonseed oil, canola oil, soybean oil, etc.
- Refined grains like pasta (having refined wheat), white bread, etc.

How to the Make Mediterranean Diet Work for You

If you want to make the Mediterranean diet work for you, start slowly instead of renovating your entire way of shopping and eating, which might seem daunting. Try to eat more in the Mediterranean-style instead of entirely wiping the slate. Start following the strategies below one by one, which will make the Mediterranean diet work for you.

Top Hints of Success

The Mediterranean diet has been credited with a lot of health benefits that can be easily gained by simple tricks. The following hints and tips will ensure that you are following the Mediterranean diet perfectly.

Doubling or Tripling Your Fruits & Veggies

A high intake of fruits and veggies is always beneficial for health. Numerous researches prove that any plant-heavy diet plan has far better health benefits than any other diet plan. Lower risk of cancer and cardiovascular diseases is associated with high fruits and veggies consumption.

Start Using Olive Oil

The major step for a successful Mediterranean diet is to eradicate all kinds of butters, oils and margarines by substituting it with olive oil. Beneficial monosaturated fats in olive oil produce HDL cholesterol, which is credited with averting heart issues.

Start Loving Legumes

Legumes are the richest protein resource included in the Mediterranean diet, being credited as the perfect dietary fiber source available. A single cup of navy beans has a high amount of protein and dietary fibers, so eat more of them.

Consume Enough Seafood & Fish

Seafood and fish are high in vitamin B & D, proteins, and selenium and is known to lower the risk of death by 12 percent according to a study. One should preferably consume fatty fish.

Increase Seasoning

The Mediterranean diet is very dependent on seasonings and herbs, which are antioxidants and can avoid various diseases. Garlic has nutrients that promote healthy immune functioning and lower the risk of cancer and bad cholesterol.

Eat Pasta

Pasta is made from durum and is less likely to elevate your blood sugar levels. In order to slow down absorption, you can combine pasta and olive oil.

Use Fruit as Dessert

Fruits are high in fiber, low in fat, and also have perfect antioxidants. Lower risk of diabetes and heart strokes is associated with consuming whole fruits. You can use fruits as desserts or even snack on them between meals.

Socializing Your Eating Habits

You must prefer to eat with your family and loved ones instead of eating alone to have a better taste of food and life.

Limit Meat Consumption

Apart from religious events, the regular Mediterranean diet does not have a high meat content. Grass-fed and pasture-raised meat that comprises of a higher amount of CLA and Omega-3 fatty acids is used.

Mediterranean Diet Recipes

Breakfast Recipes

Yogurt Pancakes

Yield	Preparation Time	Cooking Time
6 servings	15 minutes	24 minutes

Ingredients:

- ½ cup all-purpose flour
- 1 cup old-fashioned oats
- 2 tablespoons flax seeds
- 1 teaspoon baking soda
- Salt, as required
- 2 tablespoons agave syrup
- 2 large eggs
- 2 cups plain Greek yogurt
- 2 tablespoons canola oil

Directions:

1. In a blender, add the flour, oats, flax seeds, baking soda, and salt and pulse until well combined.
2. Transfer the mixture into a large bowl.

3. Add the remaining ingredients except the oil and mix until well combined.
4. Set aside for about twenty minutes before cooking.
5. Heat a large nonstick skillet over medium heat and grease with a little oil.
6. Add ¼ cup of the mixture and cook for about two minutes or until the bottom becomes golden brown.
7. Carefully flip to the other side and cook for about two minutes more.
8. Repeat with the remaining mixture.

Nutrition Information per Serving:

Calories	Fat	Carbohydrates	Protein
245	9 g	29.1 g	10 g

Eggs in Tomato Sauce

Yield	Preparation Time	Cooking Time
4 servings	15 minutes	50 minutes

Ingredients:

- 2 tablespoons butter
- 4 small yellow onions, sliced
- ½ cup chopped finely plum tomatoes
- 1 garlic clove, minced
- 4 large eggs
- 3 ounces feta cheese, crumbled
- Salt and ground black pepper, as required
- 2 tablespoons minced fresh dill

Directions:

1. In a large cast iron skillet, melt the butter over medium-low heat and stir in the onions, spreading in an even layer.
2. Reduce the heat to low and cook for about thirty minutes, stirring after every five to ten minutes.
3. Add the sun-dried tomatoes and garlic and cook for about two to three minutes, stirring frequently.
4. With the spoon, spread the mixture in an even layer.
5. Carefully crack the eggs over the onion mixture and sprinkle with the feta cheese, salt, and black pepper.
6. Cover the pan tightly and cook for about ten to fifteen minutes or until desired doneness of the eggs.
7. Serve hot with the garnishing of the parsley.

Nutrition Information per Serving:

Calories	Fat	Carbohydrates	Protein
216	15.4 g	9.8 g	10.7 g

Date Smoothie

Yield	Preparation Time	Cooking Time
18 servings	15 minutes	0

Ingredients:

- 6 Medjool dates, pitted and chopped roughly
- 1 cup plain Greek yogurt
- 2 tablespoons almond butter
- 1 cup fresh apple juice
- ½ cup ice cubes

Directions:

1. In a high-speed blender, add all of the ingredients and pulse until smooth and creamy.
2. Transfer the smoothie into two serving glasses and serve.

Calories	Fat	Carbohydrates	Protein
482	10.7 g	88.6 g	13.5 g

Veggie Omelet

Yield	Preparation Time	Cooking Time
4 servings	15 minutes	15 minutes

Ingredients:

- 1 teaspoon olive oil
- 2 cups fresh sliced thinly fennel bulbs
- ¼ cup canned, rinsed, drained, and chopped artichoke hearts
- ¼ cup pitted and chopped green olives
- 1 Roma tomato, chopped
- 6 eggs
- Salt and ground black pepper, as required
- ½ cup crumbled goat cheese

Directions:

1. Preheat the oven to 325 degrees F.
2. In a large ovenproof skillet, heat the oil over medium-high heat and sauté the fennel bulb for about five minutes.
3. Stir in the artichoke, olives and tomato and cook for about three minutes.
4. Meanwhile, in a bowl, add the eggs, salt, and black pepper and beat until well combined.
5. Place the egg mixture over veggie mixture and stir to combine.
6. Cook for about two minutes.
7. Sprinkle with the goat cheese evenly, and immediately transfer the skillet into the oven.
8. Bake for about five minutes or until eggs are set completely.
9. Remove the skillet from oven and transfer the omelet onto a platter.
10. Cut into desired sized wedges and serve.

Nutrition Information per Serving:

Calories	Fat	Carbohydrates	Protein
266	18.8 g	7.5 g	18.1 g

Veggie Muffins

Yield	Preparation Time	Cooking Time
8 servings	15 minutes	12 minutes

Ingredients:

- ¼ cup half-and-half
- 6 large eggs
- Salt and freshly ground black pepper, to taste
- ½ cup drained and chopped sun-dried tomatoes in oil
- 1/3 cup drained, pitted, and quartered canned Kalamata olives
- ¼ cup drained and chopped bottled sweet red peppers
- ¼ cup drained and sliced thinly canned artichokes in oil
- ¼ cup shredded Asiago cheese
- ¼ cup crumbled feta cheese
1. ¼ cup chopped fresh parsley

Directions:

25

1. Preheat the oven to 375 degrees F. Grease twenty-four cups of mini muffin tins.
2. In a bowl, add the half-and-half, eggs, salt, and black pepper and beat well.
3. In another large bowl, mix together the vegetables and Asiago cheese.
4. Place the egg mixture into prepared muffin cups about three-quarters full.
5. Place the vegetables mixture over the egg mixture evenly and top with remaining egg mixture.
6. Sprinkle with feta and parsley evenly.
7. Bake for about ten to twelve minutes or until the eggs are done completely.

Nutritional Information per Serving:

Calories	Fat	Carbohydrates	Protein
92	6.5 g	2.4 g	6.3 g

Soup Recipes

Mixed Veggie Soup

Yield	Preparation Time	Cooking Time
8 servings	20 minutes	25 minutes

Ingredients:

- 8 carrots peeled and chopped
- 4 small zucchinis, chopped
- 4 small onions, chopped
- 2 (14 ounce) cans diced tomatoes with juice
- 1 leek, chopped
- 2 garlic cloves, minced
- 1 teaspoon ground cumin
- ¼ teaspoon cayenne pepper
- ¼ teaspoon paprika
- Salt and ground black pepper, as required
- 4 ¼ cups vegetable broth
- 1 whole-meal bread slice, toasted and cut up into small croutons

Directions:

1. In a large soup pan, add all of the ingredients except the croutons and bring to a boil.
2. Reduce the heat to low and simmer, partially covered, for about twenty minutes.
3. Remove from the heat and set aside to cool slightly.
4. In a blender, add the soup in batches and pulse until smooth.
5. Return the pureed mixture into the pan over medium heat and simmer for about three to four minutes.
6. Serve hot with the topping of croutons.

Nutritional Information per Serving:

Calories	Fat	Carbohydrates	Protein
87	0.5 g	58.19 g	2.9 g

Lentil & Spinach Soup

Yield	Preparation Time	Cooking Time
6 servings	20 minutes	1 ¼ hours

Ingredients:

- 2 tablespoons olive oil
- 2 carrots, peeled and chopped
- 2 celery stalks, chopped
- 2 sweet onions, chopped
- 3 garlic cloves, minced
- 1 ½ cups brown lentils, rinsed
- 1 (14 ½ ounce) can diced tomatoes
- ¼ teaspoon dried crushed basil
- ¼ teaspoon dried crushed oregano
- ¼ teaspoon dried crushed thyme
- 1 teaspoon ground cumin
- ½ teaspoon ground coriander
- ½ teaspoon paprika
- 6 cups vegetable broth

- 3 cups chopped fresh spinach
- Salt and freshly ground black pepper, to taste
- 2 tablespoons fresh lemon juice

Directions:

1. In a large soup pan, heat the oil over medium heat and sauté carrot, celery, and onion for about four to five minutes.
2. Add the garlic; sauté for about one minute.
3. Add the lentils and sauté for about two to three minutes.
4. Stir in the tomatoes, herbs, spices, and broth and bring to a boil.
5. Reduce the heat to low and simmer, partially covered for about forty-five to sixty minutes.
6. Stir in the spinach, salt, and black pepper, and cook for about three to four minutes.
7. Stir in the lemon juice and serve hot.

Nutritional Information per Serving:

Calories	Fat	Carbohydrates	Protein
204	6.7 g	24.2 g	12.7 g

Chicken & Pasta Soup

Yield	Preparation Time	Cooking Time
8 servings	20 minutes	25 minutes

Ingredients:

- 2 tablespoons olive oil
- 1 ½ pounds skinless, boneless chicken breasts, cubed into ¾-inch size
- 1 tablespoon Greek seasoning
- Salt and ground black pepper, as required
- 1 large onion, chopped finely
- 1 carrot, peeled and chopped
- 1 garlic clove, minced
- ¼ cup white wine
- ¼ cup chopped sun-dried tomatoes
- 1 tablespoon drained capers
- 1 ½ teaspoons minced fresh oregano
- 1 ½ teaspoons minced fresh basil
- 7 cups chicken broth
- 1 ½ cups uncooked pasta

- 2 tablespoons fresh lemon juice
- 2 teaspoons chopped finely fresh parsley

Directions:

1. In a Dutch oven, heat the oil over medium heat, and cook the chicken breasts with Greek seasoning, salt, and black pepper for about four to five minutes or until golden brown from both sides.
2. With a slotted spoon, transfer the chicken breasts onto a plate and set aside.
3. In the same pan, add the scallions and garlic, and sauté for about one minute.
4. Add the wine and remove the browned bits from the bottom of pan.
5. Stir in the cooked chicken, tomatoes, capers, oregano, basil, and broth and bring to a boil.
6. Reduce the heat to low and simmer covered for about fifteen minutes.
7. Increase the heat to medium and again bring to a boil.
8. Stir in the pasta and cook for about eight to ten minutes or until desired doneness of the pasta.
9. Stir in the lemon juice and parsley and serve hot.

Nutritional Information per Serving:

Calories	Fat	Carbohydrates	Protein
306	8.3 g	28.4 g	27.5 g

Lamb, Lentils & Chickpeas Soup

Yield	Preparation Time	Cooking Time
8 servings	20 minutes	2 ¼ hours

Ingredients:

- 1 ½ pounds boneless lamb shoulder, cubed
- Salt and ground black pepper, as required
- 2 tablespoons olive oil
- 1 onion, chopped
- 2 garlic cloves, chopped
- 2 tablespoons tomato paste
- 2 teaspoons sweet paprika
- 1 ½ teaspoons ground cumin
- ½ teaspoon ground cloves
- 2 (14 ounce) cans diced tomatoes
- 4 cups chicken broth
- 2 (14 ounce) cans brown lentils, rinsed and drained
- 2 (14 ounce) cans chickpeas, rinsed and drained
- ½ cup chopped fresh parsley

Directions:

1. Season the lamb cubes with salt and black pepper evenly.
2. In a large pan, heat the oil over medium-high heat and sear the lamb cubes in two batches for about four to five minutes.
3. With a slotted spoon, transfer the lamb cubes into a bowl.
4. In the same pan, add the onion and garlic over medium heat and sauté for about three to four minutes.
5. Add the cooked lamb, tomato paste and spices and cook for about one minute.
6. Stir in the tomatoes and broth and bring to a boil.
7. Reduce the heat to low and simmer, covered for about one hour.
8. Stir in the lentils and chickpeas and simmer, covered for about thirty minutes.
9. Uncover and simmer for about thirty minutes more.
10. Stir in the salt and black pepper and remove from the heat.
11. Serve hot with the garnishing of parsley.

Nutritional Information per Serving:

Calories	Fat	Carbohydrates	Protein
418	12.9 g	36.1 g	39.4 g

Tomato Soup

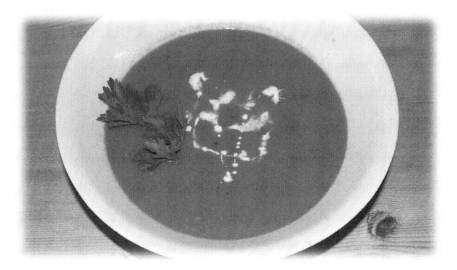

Yield	Preparation Time	Cooking Time
8 servings	15 minutes	28 minutes

- 3 tablespoons olive oil
- 2 medium yellow onions, sliced thinly
- Salt, as required
- 3 teaspoons curry powder, 1 teaspoon ground cumin
- 1 teaspoon ground coriander, ½ teaspoon red pepper flakes
- 1 (15 ounce) can diced tomatoes with juice
- 1 (28 ounce) can plum tomatoes with juices
- 5 ½ cups vegetable broth
- ½ cup crumbled ricotta cheese

Directions:

1. In a Dutch oven, heat the oil over medium-low heat and cook the onion with one teaspoon of the salt for about ten to twelve minutes, stirring occasionally.
2. Stir in the curry powder, cumin, coriander, and red pepper flakes and sauté for about one minute.
3. Stir in the tomatoes with juices and broth and simmer for about fifteen minutes.
4. Remove from the heat and with a hand blender, blend the soup until smooth.
5. Serve immediately with the topping of ricotta cheese.

Calories	Fat	Carbohydrates	Protein
140	7.9 g	11.8 g	7.2 g

Salad Recipes

Watermelon Salad

Yield	Preparation Time	Cooking Time
4 servings	15 minutes	0

Ingredients:
For Vinaigrette:

- 2 tablespoons fresh lime juice
- 2 tablespoons honey
- 1 tablespoon olive oil
- Pinch of salt

For Salad:

- 1 (5 pound) watermelon, peeled and cut into cubes
- 2 cups cubed cucumber
- 3 tablespoons torn fresh mint leaves
- ½ cup crumbled feta cheese

Directions:

1. For vinaigrette: in a small bowl, all the ingredients and beat until well combined.
2. In a large bowl, add the watermelon, cucumber, and mint and mix.
3. Place in the vinaigrette and gently toss to coat.
4. Top with the feta cheese and serve.

Calories	Fat	Carbohydrates	Protein
292	8.3 g	54.3 g	6.5 g

Fresh Veggie Salad

Yield	Preparation Time	Cooking Time
6 servings	15 minutes	0

Ingredients:
- 2 cucumbers, peeled and chopped
- 3 large Roma tomatoes, chopped
- 1 cup pitted Kalamata olives
- 1 large avocado, peeled, pitted and chopped
- 8 cups fresh baby spinach
- ¼ cup extra-virgin olive oil
- 2 tablespoons fresh lemon juice
- 1 ½ teaspoons dried oregano, crushed
- Salt and ground black pepper, as required
- 1 cup crumbled feta cheese

Directions:
1. In a large serving bowl, add all of the ingredients except feta and toss to coat well.
2. Top with the feta and serve immediately.

Calories	Fat	Carbohydrates	Protein
140	7.9 g	11.8 g	7.2 g

Chickpeas Salad

Yield	Preparation Time	Cooking Time
6 servings	15 minutes	0

Ingredients:

For Salad:

- 2 (15 ounce) cans chickpeas, rinsed and drained
- 2 ½ cups chopped tomatoes
- 2 cups chopped cucumber
- ½ cup pitted Kalamata olives
- 1 red onion, chopped
- ½ cup chopped fresh mint leaves
- ½ cup chopped fresh parsley leaves

For Dressing:

- ¼ cup extra-virgin olive oil
- 2 tablespoons fresh lemon juice
- 2 tablespoons white wine vinegar
- 1 garlic clove, minced
- 1 teaspoon ground sumac

- ½ teaspoon crushed red pepper flakes
- Salt and ground black pepper, as required

Directions:

1. For the salad: in a large serving bowl, add all of the ingredients and mix.
2. For the dressing: in another bowl, add all of the ingredients and beat until well combined.
3. Place the dressing over the salad and gently toss to coat.
4. Set aside for about thirty minutes.
5. Gently stir the salad and serve.

Nutritional Information per Serving:

Calories	Fat	Carbohydrates	Protein
238	12.7 g	23.7 g	9.2 g

Chicken Salad

Yield	Preparation Time	Cooking Time
6 servings	20 minutes	0

For Salad:
- 3 cups cubed cooked chicken breast
- 1 ½ cups chopped tomatoes
- ½ cup pitted Kalamata olives
- ½ cup pitted green olives
- ½ cup chopped finely red onion
- ½ cup crumbled feta cheese

For Dressing:
- ¼ cup olive oil
- 2 tablespoons tarragon vinegar
- 1 tablespoon fresh lemon juice
- 1 tablespoon minced fresh tarragon
- 1 ½ teaspoons Dijon mustard
- Salt and ground black pepper, as required

Directions:
1. For the salad: in a large serving bowl, add all of the ingredients and mix well.
2. For the dressing: in another bowl, add all of the ingredients and beat until well combined.
3. Place the dressing over the salad and gently toss to coat.
4. Refrigerate to chill before serving.

Calories	Fat	Carbohydrates	Protein
284	19.1 g	4.9 g	23.5 g

Tuna Salad

Yield	Preparation Time	Cooking Time
6 servings	20 minutes	0

Ingredients:

For Vinaigrette:

- 3 tablespoons fresh lime juice
- 1/3 cup extra-virgin olive oil
- 2 ½ teaspoons Dijon mustard
- 1 teaspoon grated fresh lime zest
- ½ teaspoon crushed red pepper flakes
- Salt and ground black pepper, as required

For Salad:

- 3 (5 ounce) cans tuna in olive oil
- 1 red onion, chopped
- 2 cucumbers, sliced
- 1 large tomato, sliced
- ½ cup pitted Kalamata olives
- 8 cups torn lettuce leaves
- ¼ cup fresh basil leaves

Directions:

1. For the vinaigrette: in a bowl, add all of the ingredients and beat until well combined.
2. For the salad: in a large serving bowl, add all of the ingredients and mix.
3. Place the dressing over the salad and gently toss to coat.
4. Refrigerate, covered for about thirty to forty minutes before serving.

Nutritional Information per Serving:

Calories	Fat	Carbohydrates	Protein
263	16.6 g	9.7 g	21.9 g

Fish & Seafood Recipes

Salmon with Capers

Yield	Preparation Time	Cooking Time
4 servings	15 minutes	8 minutes

Ingredients:

- 2 tablespoons olive oil
- 4 (6 ounce) salmon fillets
- 2 tablespoons capers
- Salt and ground black pepper as required
- 4 lemon wedges

Directions:

1. In a large skillet, heat the oil over high heat and cook the salmon fillets for about three minutes.
2. Sprinkle the salmon fillets with capers, salt, and black pepper.
3. Flip the salmon fillets and cook for about five minutes or until browned.
4. Serve with the garnishing of lemon wedges.

Calories	Fat	Carbohydrates	Protein
286	17.5 g	0.4 g	33.1 g

Tilapia in Herb Sauce

Yield	Preparation Time	Cooking Time
4 servings	15 minutes	14 minutes

Ingredients:

- 2 (14 ounce) cans diced tomatoes with basil and garlic, undrained
- 1/3 cup fresh parsley, chopped and divided
- ¼ teaspoon dried oregano
- ½ teaspoon red pepper flakes, crushed
- 4 (6 ounce) tilapia fillets
- 2 tablespoons fresh lemon juice
- 2/3 cup crumbled feta cheese

Directions:

1. Preheat the oven to 400 degrees F.
2. In a shallow baking dish, add the tomatoes, a quarter of a cup of the parsley, oregano, and red pepper flakes and mix until well combined.
3. Arrange the tilapia fillets over the tomato mixture in a single layer and drizzle with the lemon juice.
4. Place some tomato mixture over the tilapia fillets and sprinkle with the feta cheese evenly.
5. Bake for about twelve to fourteen minutes.
6. Serve hot with the garnishing of remaining parsley.

Calories	Fat	Carbohydrates	Protein
246	7.4 g	9.4 g	37.2 g

Salmon with Avocado Cream

Yield	Preparation Time	Cooking Time
4 servings	15 minutes	8 minutes

Ingredients:

For Avocado Cream:

- 2 avocados, peeled, pitted, and chopped
- 1 cup plain Greek yogurt
- 2 garlic cloves, chopped
- 3-4 tablespoons fresh lime juice
- Salt and ground black pepper, as required

For Salmon:

- 2 teaspoons ground cumin
- 2 teaspoons red chili powder
- 2 teaspoons paprika
- 2 teaspoons garlic powder
- Salt and ground black pepper, as required
- 4 (6 ounce) skinless salmon fillets
- 2 tablespoons butter

Directions:

1. **For the avocado cream:** in a food processor, add all of the ingredients and pulse until smooth.
2. In a small bowl, mix together the spices.
3. Coat the salmon fillets with spice mixture evenly.
4. In a nonstick skillet, melt butter over medium-high heat and cook salmon fillets for about three minutes.
5. Flip and cook for about four to five minutes or until desired doneness.
6. Transfer the salmon fillets onto serving plates.
7. Top with avocado cream and serve.

Nutritional Information per Serving:

Calories	Fat	Carbohydrates	Protein
557	38.5 g	14.9 g	39.2 g

Grilled Salmon

Yield	Preparation Time	Cooking Time
4 servings	15 minutes	12 minutes

Ingredients:

- ½ cup plain Greek yogurt
- 3 garlic cloves, minced
- 2 tablespoons minced fresh dill
- 2 tablespoons fresh lemon juice
- 1 tablespoon extra-virgin olive oil
- 1 ½ teaspoons ground coriander
- 1 ½ teaspoons ground cumin
- Salt and ground black pepper, as required
- 4 (6 ounce) skinless salmon fillets
- 2 tablespoons fresh basil leaves

Directions:

1. In a large bowl, add all of the ingredients except the salmon and basil and mix well.
2. Transfer half of the yogurt mixture into another bowl and reserve for serving.
3. In the large bowl of the remaining yogurt mixture, add the salmon fillets and coat with the mixture well.
4. Refrigerate for about twenty-five to thirty minutes, flipping once half way through.
5. Preheat the grill to medium-high heat. Lightly grease the grill grate.
6. Remove the salmon fillets from the bowl and, with the paper towels, discard the excess yogurt mixture.
7. Grill the salmon fillets for about four to six minutes per side.
8. Serve with the topping of the reserved yogurt mixture and basil.

Nutritional Information per Serving:

Calories	Fat	Carbohydrates	Protein
365	22.2 g	4.3 g	35.6 g

Tilapia with Capers

Yield	Preparation Time	Cooking Time
4 servings	15 minutes	15 minutes

Ingredients:

- 1 ½ teaspoons paprika
- 1 ½ teaspoons ground cumin
- Salt and ground black pepper, as required
- 2 shallots, chopped finely
- 3 garlic cloves, minced
- 2 tablespoons fresh lemon juice
- 1 ½ tablespoons butter, melted
- 1 pound tilapia, cut into 8 pieces
- ¼ cup capers

Directions:

1. Preheat the oven to 375 degrees F. Line a rimmed baking sheet with a greased parchment paper.
2. In a small bowl, mix together the paprika, cumin, salt, and black pepper.
3. In another small bowl, add the butter, shallots, garlic, lemon juice, and butter and mix until well combined.
4. Season the tilapia fillets with the spice mixture evenly and coat with the butter mixture generously.
5. Arrange the tilapia fillets onto the prepared baking sheet and top with the capers.
6. Bake for about ten to fifteen minutes or until desired doneness of fish.
7. Serve hot.

Nutritional Information per Serving:

Calories	Fat	Carbohydrates	Protein
150	5.8 g	3.6 g	22 g

Almond Crusted Tilapia

Yield	Preparation Time	Cooking Time
4 servings	15 minutes	10 minutes

- 1 cup almonds, chopped finely and divided
- ¼ cup ground flaxseed
- 4 (6 ounce) tilapia fillets
- Salt, to taste
- 2 tablespoons olive oil

Directions:

1. In a shallow bowl, mix together a half a cup of almonds and ground flaxseed.
2. Season the tilapia fillets with the salt evenly.
3. Now, coat the fillets with the almond mixture evenly.
4. In a large heavy skillet, heat the oil over medium heat and cook the tilapia fillets for about four minutes per side.
5. Transfer the tilapia fillets onto a serving plate.
6. In the same skillet, add the remaining almonds and cook for about one minute, stirring frequently.
7. Remove the almonds from the heat and sprinkle over fish.
8. Serve warm.

Calories	Fat	Carbohydrates	Protein
374	22.6 g	7.1 g	38 g

Grilled Prawns

Yield	Preparation Time	Cooking Time
4 servings	15 minutes	2 minutes

Ingredients:

- 3 ¼ pounds large prawns, peeled and deveined, with tails intact
- 6 large garlic cloves, minced
- 1/3 cup extra-virgin olive oil
- 2 tablespoons fresh lemon juice
- Salt and ground black pepper, as required

Directions:

1. Preheat the barbecue grill to high heat. Lightly grease the grill grate.
2. In a bowl, add all the ingredients and toss to coat well.
3. Grill the prawns for about one minute per side.
4. Serve warm.

Nutritional Information per Serving:

Calories	Fat	Carbohydrates	Protein
295	11.6 g	3.6 g	42.1 g

Halibut with Olives & Tomatoes

Yield	Preparation Time	Cooking Time
4 servings	15 minutes	40 minutes

Ingredients:

- 1 onion, chopped
- 1 large tomato, chopped
- 1 (5 ounce) jar pitted kalamata olives
- ¼ cup capers
- ¼ cup olive oil
- 1 tablespoon fresh lemon juice
- Salt and ground black pepper, as required
- 4 (6 ounce) halibut fillets
- 1 tablespoon Greek seasoning

Directions:

1. Preheat the oven to 350 degrees F.
2. In a bowl, add the onion, tomato, olives, capers, oil, lemon juice, salt, and black pepper and mix well.
3. Season the halibut fillets with the Greek seasoning and arrange onto a large piece of foil.
4. Top the fillets with the tomato mixture.
5. Carefully, fold all of the edges to create a large packet.
6. Arrange the packet onto a baking sheet.
7. Bake for about thirty to forty minutes.
8. Serve hot.

Nutritional Information per Serving:

Calories	Fat	Carbohydrates	Protein
399	20.7 g	8.2 g	48 g

Cod in Tomato Sauce

Yield	Preparation Time	Cooking Time
5 servings	15 minutes	35 minutes

Ingredients:

- 1 teaspoon dried dill weed
- 2 teaspoons sumac
- 2 teaspoons ground coriander
- 1½ teaspoons ground cumin
- 1 teaspoon ground turmeric
- 2 tablespoons olive oil
- 1 large sweet onion, chopped
- 8 garlic cloves, chopped
- 2 jalapeño peppers, chopped
- 5 medium tomatoes, chopped
- 3 tablespoons tomato paste
- 2 tablespoons fresh lime juice
- ½ cup water
- Salt and ground black pepper, as required
- 5 (6 ounce) cod fillets

Directions:

1. For the spice mixture: in a small bowl, add the dill weed and spices and mix well.
2. In a large, deep skillet, heat the oil over medium-high heat and sauté the onion for about two minutes.
3. Add the garlic and jalapeno and sauté for about two minutes.
4. Stir in the tomatoes, tomato paste, lime juice, water, half of the spice mixture, salt and pepper and bring to a boil.
5. Reduce the heat to medium-low and cook covered for about ten minutes, stirring occasionally.
6. Meanwhile, season the cod fillets with the remaining spice mixture, salt, and pepper evenly.
7. Place the fish fillets into the skillet and gently press into the tomato mixture.
8. Increase the heat to medium-high and cook for about two minutes.
9. Reduce the heat to medium and cook, covered for about ten to fifteen minutes or until desired doneness of the fish.
10. Serve hot.

Nutritional Information per Serving:

Calories	Fat	Carbohydrates	Protein
285	7.7 g	12.5 g	41.4 g

Tuna with Olives Sauce

Yield	Preparation Time	Cooking Time
4 servings	15 minutes	10 minutes

Ingredients:

- 4 (6 ounce) (1-inch thick) tuna steaks
- 2 tablespoons extra-virgin olive oil, divided
- Salt and ground black pepper, as required
- 2 garlic cloves, minced
- 1 cup chopped fresh tomatoes
- 1 cup dry white wine
- 2/3 cup pitted and sliced green olives
- ¼ cup drained capers
- 2 tablespoons chopped fresh thyme
- 1 ½ tablespoons grated fresh lemon zest
- 2 tablespoons fresh lemon juice
- 3 tablespoons chopped fresh parsley

Directions:

1. Preheat the grill to high heat. Grease the grill grate.
2. Coat the tuna steaks with one tablespoon of the oil and sprinkle with salt and black pepper.
3. Set aside for about five minutes.
4. For the sauce: in a small skillet, heat the remaining oil over medium heat and sauté the garlic for about one minute.
5. Add the tomatoes and cook for about two minutes.
6. Stir in the wine and bring to a boil.
7. Add the remaining ingredients except the parsley, and cook uncovered for about five minutes.
8. Stir in the parsley, salt, and black pepper and remove from the heat.
9. Meanwhile, grill the tuna steaks over direct heat for about one to two minutes per side.
10. Serve the tuna steaks hot with the topping of sauce.

Nutritional Information per Serving:

Calories	Fat	Carbohydrates	Protein
468	20.4 g	7.3 g	52.1 g

Mussels in Wine Sauce

Yield	Preparation Time	Cooking Time
6 servings	15 minutes	18 minutes

Ingredients:

- 1 tablespoon olive oil
- 2 celery stalks, chopped
- 1 onion, chopped
- 4 garlic cloves, minced
- ½ teaspoon crushed dried oregano
- 1 (15 ounce) can diced tomatoes
- 1 teaspoon honey
- 1 teaspoon crushed red pepper flakes
- 2 pounds mussels, cleaned
- 2 cups white wine
- Salt and ground black pepper, as required
- ¼ cup chopped fresh basil

Directions:

1. In a large skillet, heat the oil over medium heat and sauté the celery, onion, and garlic for about five minutes.
2. Add the tomato, honey, and red pepper flakes and cook for about ten minutes.
3. Meanwhile, in a large pan, add mussels and wine and bring to a boil.
4. Simmer, covered for about ten minutes.
5. Transfer the mussel mixture into tomato mixture and stir to combine.
6. Season with salt and black pepper and remove from the heat.
7. Serve hot with the garnishing of basil.

Nutritional Information per Serving:

Calories	Fat	Carbohydrates	Protein
244	6 g	14.3 g	19.1 g

Octopus in Honey Sauce

Yield	Preparation Time	Cooking Time
8 servings	20 minutes	1 hour 25 minutes

Ingredients:

- 2 ¼ pounds fresh octopus, washed
- 1 bay leaf
- 1/3 cup water
- 4 tablespoons olive oil
- 2 onions, chopped finely
- Pinch of saffron threads, crushed
- 1 garlic clove, chopped finely
- 1 tablespoon tomato paste
- 1 (14 ounce) can diced tomatoes
- 1 tablespoon honey
- ¾ cup red wine
- Salt and ground black pepper, as required
- ¼ cup chopped fresh basil leaves

Directions:

1. Remove the eyes of the octopus and cut out the beak.
2. Then clean the head thoroughly.
3. In a deep pan, add the octopus, bay leaf, and water over medium heat and cook for about twenty minutes.
4. Add the wine and simmer for about fifty minutes.
5. Meanwhile, for the sauce: in a skillet, heat the oil over medium heat and sauté the onions and saffron for about three to four minutes.
6. Add the garlic and tomato paste and sauté for about one to two minutes.
7. Stir in the tomatoes and honey and simmer for about ten minutes.
8. Transfer the sauce into the pan of octopus and cooking for about fifteen minutes.
9. Serve hot with the garnishing of basil.

Nutritional Information per Serving:

Calories	Fat	Carbohydrates	Protein
319	10.1 g	13.8 g	38.4 g

Seafood Paella

Yield	Preparation Time	Cooking Time
4 servings	20 minutes	40 minutes

Ingredients:

- 1 tablespoon extra-virgin olive oil
- 1 red bell pepper, seeded and chopped finely
- 1 large yellow onion, chopped finely
- 4 garlic cloves, minced
- 1 ½ cups short grain rice
- ½ teaspoon ground turmeric
- 1 teaspoon paprika
- 14 ounces canned diced tomatoes
- 2 pinches saffron threads, crushed
- 3 cups chicken broth
- 12 mussels, cleaned
- 12 large shrimp, peeled and deveined

- ½ cup frozen peas, thawed
- ¼ cup chopped fresh parsley
- 1 lemon, cut into wedges

Directions:

1. In a deep pan, heat the oil over medium-high heat and sauté the bell pepper, onion, and garlic for about three minutes.
2. Add the rice, turmeric, and paprika and stir to combine.
3. Stir in the tomatoes, saffron, and broth and bring to a boil.
4. Reduce the heat to low and simmer covered for about twenty minutes.
5. Place the mussels, shrimp and peas on top and simmer, covered for about ten to fifteen minutes.
6. Serve hot with the garnishing of parsley and lemon wedges.

Nutritional Information per Serving:

Calories	Fat	Carbohydrates	Protein
456	6.8 g	76.7 g	21.1 g

Seafood Stew

Yield	Preparation Time	Cooking Time
4 servings	20 minutes	25 minutes

Ingredients:

- 2 tablespoons olive oil
- 1 medium onion, chopped finely
- 2 garlic cloves, minced
- ¼ teaspoon crushed red pepper flakes
- ½ pound plum tomatoes, seeded and chopped
- 1/3 cup white wine
- 1 cup clam juice
- 1 tablespoon tomato paste
- Salt, as required
- 1 pound snapper fillets, cubed into 1-inch size
- 1 pound large shrimp, peeled and deveined
- ½ pound sea scallops

- 1/3 cup minced fresh parsley
- 1 teaspoon grated finely fresh lemon zest

Directions:

1. In a large Dutch oven, heat the oil over medium heat and sauté the onion for about three to four minutes.
2. Add the garlic and red pepper flakes and sauté for about one minute.
3. Add the tomatoes and cook for about two minutes.
4. Stir in the wine, clam juice, tomato paste, and salt and bring to a boil.
5. Reduce the heat to low and simmer, covered for about ten minutes.
6. Stir in the seafood and simmer, covered for about six to eight minutes.
7. Stir in the parsley and remove from heat.
8. Serve hot with the garnishing of lemon zest.

Nutritional Information per Serving:

Calories	Fat	Carbohydrates	Protein
313	7.8 g	11.6 g	44.3 g

Garlicky Shrimp

Yield	Preparation Time	Cooking Time
4 servings	15 minutes	6 minutes

Ingredients:
- 2 tablespoons olive oil
- 3 garlic cloves, sliced
- 1 pound shrimp, peeled and deveined
- 1 tablespoon chopped fresh rosemary
- ½ teaspoon crushed red pepper flakes
- Salt and ground black pepper, as required
- 1 tablespoon fresh lemon juice

Directions:
1. In a large skillet, heat the oil over medium heat and sauté the garlic slices or about two minutes or until golden brown.
2. With a slotted spoon, transfer the garlic slices into a bowl.
3. In the same skillet, add the shrimp, rosemary, red pepper flakes, salt, and black pepper and cook for about three to four minutes, stirring frequently.
4. Stir in the lemon juice and remove from the heat.
5. Serve hot with a topping of the garlic slices.

Calories	Fat	Carbohydrates	Protein
202	9.1 g	3.2 g	26.1 g

Meat & Poultry Recipes

Spiced Lamb Chops

Yield	Preparation Time	Cooking Time
8 servings	15 minutes	7 minutes

Ingredients:

- 1 tablespoon chopped fresh mint leaves
- 1 teaspoon garlic paste
- 1 teaspoon ground allspice
- ½ teaspoon ground nutmeg
- ½ teaspoon ground green cardamom
- ¼ teaspoon hot paprika
- Salt and ground black pepper, as required
- 4 tablespoons olive oil
- 2 tablespoons fresh lemon juice
- 2 racks of lamb chops, trimmed and separated into 16 chops

Directions:

1. In a large bowl, add all the ingredients except the chops and mix until well combined.
2. Add the chops and coat with the mixture generously.
3. Refrigerate to marinate for about five to six hours.
4. Preheat the gas grill to high heat. Grease the grill grate.
5. Grill the lamb chops for about six to seven minutes, flipping once halfway through.
6. Serve hot.

Nutritional Information per Serving:

Calories	Fat	Carbohydrates	Protein
587	20.7 g	0.5 g	63.6 g

Leg of Lamb with Potatoes

Yield	Preparation Time	Cooking Time
8 servings	20 minutes	15 minutes

Ingredients:

For Lamb & Potatoes:

- 1 (4 pound) bone-in leg of lamb, fat trimmed
- Salt and ground black pepper, as required
- 5 garlic cloves, sliced
- 8 medium potatoes, peeled and cut into wedges
- 1 medium onion, peeled and cut into wedges
- 1 teaspoon garlic powder
- 1 teaspoon paprika
- 2 cups water

For Spice Mixture:

- ½ cup olive oil
- ¼ cup fresh lemon juice

- 5 garlic cloves, peeled
- 2 tablespoons dried mint
- 2 tablespoons dried oregano
- 1 tablespoon paprika
- ½ tablespoon ground nutmeg

Directions:

1. Remove the leg of lamb from the refrigerator and set aside in room temperature for about one hour before cooking.
2. For the spice mixture: in a food processor, add all of the ingredients and pulse until smooth.
3. Transfer the spice mixture into a bowl and set aside.
4. Preheat the broiler of the oven.
5. With paper towels, pat dry the leg of lamb completely.
6. With a sharp knife, make a few slits on both sides the leg of lamb and season with salt and black pepper.
7. Place the leg of lamb onto a wire rack and arrange the rack on the top oven rack.
8. Broil for about five to seven minutes per side.
9. Remove from the oven and transfer the leg of lamb onto a platter to cool slightly.
10. Now, set the oven temperature to 375 degrees F. Arrange a rack in the middle of the oven. Place a wire rack into a large roasting pan.
11. Carefully, insert the garlic slices in the slits of leg of lamb and rub with the spice mixture generously.
12. In a bowl, add the potato, onion, garlic powder, paprika, and a little salt and toss to coat well.
13. Place two cups of water into the bottom of the prepared roasting pan
14. Place the leg of lamb in the middle of the prepared roasting pan and arrange the potato and onion wedges around the lamb.
15. With a large piece of foil, cover the roasting pan.
16. Roast for about one hour.
17. Remove the foil and roast for about ten to fifteen minutes more.
18. Remove from the oven and place the leg of lamb onto a cutting board for at least twenty minutes before carving.
19. Cut into desired sized slices and serve alongside potatoes.

Calories	Fat	Carbohydrates	Protein
700	29.9 g	37.9 g	68.1 g

Lamb Koftas with Yogurt Sauce

Yield	Preparation Time	Cooking Time
6 servings	20 minutes	10 minutes

Ingredients:

For Lamb Kofta:

- 1 pound ground lamb
- 2 tablespoons fat-free plain Greek yogurt
- 2 tablespoons grated onion
- 2 teaspoons minced garlic
- 2 tablespoons minced fresh cilantro
- 1 teaspoon ground coriander
- 1 teaspoon ground cumin
- 1 teaspoon ground turmeric
- Salt and ground black pepper, as required
- 1 tablespoon olive oil

For Yogurt Sauce:

- ½ cup plain Greek yogurt
- ¼ cup chopped roasted red bell pepper
- 2 teaspoons minced garlic
- 1 teaspoon ground coriander
- 1 teaspoon ground cumin
- ½ teaspoon crushed red pepper flakes
- Salt, to taste

Directions:

1. For the Koftas: in a large bowl, add all of the ingredients except lamb and mix until well combined.
2. Make twelve equal-sized oblong patties.
3. In a large nonstick skillet, heat the oil to medium-high heat.
4. Add the patties and cook for about ten minutes or until browned on both sides, flipping occasionally.
5. Meanwhile, for the sauce: in a bowl, add all of the ingredients and mix until well combined.
6. Serve the Koftas with the yogurt sauce.

Nutritional Information per Serving:

Calories	Fat	Carbohydrates	Protein
189	8.4 g	3.8 g	23.1 g

Beef Stew

Yield	Preparation Time	Cooking Time
8 servings	20 minutes	1 hour 35 minutes

Ingredients:

- 1 tablespoon olive oil
- 2 pounds boneless beef chuck roast, cut into ¾-inch cubes
- 1 (14½ ounce) can diced tomatoes with juice
- ¼ cup quick-cooking tapioca
- 1 tablespoon honey
- 2 teaspoons ground cinnamon
- ¼ teaspoon garlic powder
- Salt and ground black pepper, as required
- ¼ cup red wine vinegar
- 2 cups beef broth
- 3 cups peeled and cubed sweet potato
- 2 medium yellow onions, cut into thin wedges
- 2 cups pitted prunes

Directions:

1. In a Dutch oven, heat one tablespoon of oil over medium-high heat and sear the beef cubes in two batches for about four to five minutes or until browned.
2. Drain off the grease from the pan.
3. Stir in the tomatoes, tapioca, honey, cinnamon, garlic powder, black pepper, vinegar, and broth and bring to a boil.
4. Reduce the heat to low and simmer covered for about one hour, stirring occasionally.
5. Stir in the onions and sweet potato and simmer covered for about twenty to thirty minutes.
6. Stir in the prunes and cook for about three to five minutes.
7. Serve hot.

Nutritional Information per Serving:

Calories	Fat	Carbohydrates	Protein
675	34.1 g	59.6 g	34.1 g

Beef & Olives Bake

Yield	Preparation Time	Cooking Time
6 servings	20 minutes	2 hours 15 minutes

Ingredients:

- 2 tablespoons olive oil
- 1 pound 10 ounces lean stewing steak, cut into large chunks
- 2 red onions, cut into thick wedges
- 3 bell peppers, seeded and cut into thick slices
- 1 ¼ pounds plum tomatoes, quartered
- 2 tablespoons sun-dried tomato paste
- 5 ounces canned green olives, drained
- 1/3 cup chopped fresh oregano
- 2 heads garlic, halved
- 1 cup red wine
- ½ cup water
- Salt and ground black pepper, as required

Directions:

1. Preheat the oven to 375 degrees F.
2. In a roasting pan, heat the oil over medium heat and sear the steak chunks in two batches for about five minutes or until browned.
3. With a slotted spoon, transfer the steak chunks into a bowl.
4. In the same roasting pan, add the onions and bell peppers and sauté for about five minutes.
5. Add the cooked steak chunks and remaining ingredients and stir to combine.
6. With a piece of foil, cover the roasting tin and bake for about one hour.
7. Remove the foil and bake for about one hour more.
8. Serve hot.

Nutritional Information per Serving:

Calories	Fat	Carbohydrates	Protein
412	15.7 g	21.5 g	40.8 g

Chicken with Caper Sauce

Yield	Preparation Time	Cooking Time
2 servings	15 minutes	15 minutes

Ingredients:

- ½ cup all-purpose flour
- Salt, to taste
- 2 (6 ounce) skinless, boneless chicken breast halves
- 2 tablespoons olive oil
- ¼ cup dry white wine
- 3 tablespoons fresh lime juice
- ¼ cup cold unsalted butter, cut into pieces
- 2 tablespoons drained capers
- ½ lime, cut into wedges

Directions:

1. In a shallow dish, mix together the flour and salt.
2. Add the chicken breasts and coat with flour mixture evenly.
3. Then, shake off the excess.
4. In a skillet, heat the oil over medium-high heat and cook the chicken breasts for about three to four minutes per side.
5. With a slotted spoon, transfer the chicken breasts onto a plate and, with a piece of foil, cover them to keep warm.
6. In the same skillet, add the wine and bring to a boil, scraping up the browned bits from the bottom of the pan.
7. Add the lemon juice and cook for about two to three minutes or until reduced by half.
8. Add the butter and cook until the sauce becomes thick, shaking the pan vigorously.
9. Remove from the heat and stir in the capers.
10. Place the caper sauce over the chicken and serve with lime wedges.

Nutritional Information per Serving:

Calories	Fat	Carbohydrates	Protein
677	43.5 g	25.2 g	41.7 g

Chicken Casserole

Yield	Preparation Time	Cooking Time
4 servings	20 minutes	50 minutes

Ingredients:

- 6 ounces dried apricots, quartered
- 6 ounces dried prunes, quartered
- 4 ounces black olives, pitted
- 2 ounces capers
- 2 garlic cloves, crushed
- 2 tablespoons minced fresh oregano
- Salt and ground black pepper, as required
- 1 bay leaf
- 2/3 cup red wine vinegar
- ¼ cup olive oil
- 4 (6 ounce) chicken drumsticks
- 3 tablespoons brown sugar
- ¾ cup white wine

Directions:

1. For the marinade: in a large baking dish, add the apricots, prunes, olives, capers, garlic, oregano, salt, black pepper, bay leaf, vinegar, and oil and mix until well combined.
2. Add the chicken breasts and coat with the marinade generously.
3. Refrigerate covered overnight.
4. Remove from the refrigerator and set aside in the room temperature for at least one hour before cooking.
5. Preheat the oven to 325 degrees F.
6. Remove the chicken breasts from the bowl and arrange in a baking dish in a single layer.
7. Spread the marinade over the chicken breasts evenly and sprinkle with the brown sugar.
8. Place the white wine around the chicken breasts.
9. Bake for about 50 minutes.
10. Serve hot.

Nutritional Information per Serving:

Calories	Fat	Carbohydrates	Protein
559	22.5 g	44.4 g	40.4 g

Chicken & Veggie Kabobs

Yield	Preparation Time	Cooking Time
8 servings	20 minutes	10 minutes

Ingredients:

- ¼ cup white vinegar
- ¼ cup fresh lemon juice
- ¼ cup olive oil
- 2 garlic cloves, minced
- ½ teaspoon crushed dried thyme
- ½ teaspoon crushed dried oregano
- 1 teaspoon ground cumin
- Salt and ground black pepper, as required
- 2 pounds skinless, boneless chicken breast, cubed into ½-inch size
- 1 medium red bell pepper, seeded and cubed into 1-inch size
- 1 medium green bell pepper, seeded and cubed into 1-inch size
- 1 zucchini, sliced
- 16 fresh mushrooms, sliced
- 16 cherry tomatoes
- 1 large onion, quartered and separated into pieces

Directions:

1. In a large bowl, add the vinegar, lemon juice, oil, garlic, dried herbs, cumin, salt, and black pepper and mix until well combined.
2. Add the chicken cubes and coat with mixture generously.
3. Refrigerate, covered to marinate for about two to four hours.
4. Preheat the outdoor grill to medium-high heat. Grease the grill grate.
5. Remove the chicken from the bowl and discard the excess marinade.
6. Thread the chicken and vegetables onto pre-soaked wooden skewers respectively.
7. Grill for about ten minutes, flipping occasionally or until desired doneness.
8. Serve hot.

Nutritional Information per Serving:

Calories	Fat	Carbohydrates	Protein
275	11.2 g	16.3 g	29.6 g

Roasted Chicken

Yield	Preparation Time	Cooking Time
4 servings	15 minutes	1 hour 35 minutes

Ingredients:

- ¼ cup extra-virgin olive oil
- 3 garlic cloves, minced
- 2 teaspoons grated finely lemon zest
- 2 teaspoons crushed dried oregano
- 1 teaspoon paprika
- 1 teaspoon cayenne pepper
- 1 teaspoon ground cumin
- ½ teaspoon ground fennel seeds
- Salt and ground black pepper, as required
- 1 (3 pound) frying chicken, neck and giblets removed

Directions:

1. In a large bowl, add all of the ingredients except the chicken and mix well.
2. Add the chicken and coat with the mixture generously.
3. Refrigerate to marinate overnight, turning occasionally.
4. Preheat the oven to 425 degrees F.
5. Remove the chicken from the bowl and arrange in a roasting pan.
6. Coat the chicken with the marinade.
7. With a kitchen string, tie the legs and tuck the wings back under the body.
8. Roast for about ten minutes.
9. Now, reduce the temperature of oven to 350 degrees F and roast for about 1 ½ hours.
10. Remove from the oven and place the chicken onto a cutting board for about ten minutes before carving.
11. Cut into desired sized pieces and serve.

Nutritional Information per Serving:

Calories	Fat	Carbohydrates	Protein
766	38.2 g	2.2 g	98.9 g

Lemony Chicken Breast

Yield	Preparation Time	Cooking Time
4 servings	15 minutes	12 minutes

- 4 (4 ounce) boneless, skinless chicken breast halves
- 3 garlic cloves, chopped finely
- 3 tablespoons chopped fresh parsley
- 3 tablespoons olive oil
- 3 tablespoons lemon juice
- 1 teaspoon paprika
- ½ teaspoon dried oregano
- Salt and ground black pepper, as required

Directions:
1. With a fork, pierce the chicken breasts several times.
2. In a large bowl, add all of the ingredients except the chicken breasts and mix until well combined.
3. Add the chicken breasts and coat with the marinade generously.
4. Refrigerate to marinate for about two to three hours.
5. Preheat the grill to medium-high heat. Grease the grill grate.
6. Remove chicken from marinade and grill for about five to six minutes per side.
7. Serve hot.

Calories	Fat	Carbohydrates	Protein
315	19.1 g	1.6 g	33.2 g

Pizza & Pasta Recipes

Veggie Pizza

Yield	Preparation Time	Cooking Time
6 servings	20 minutes	12 minutes

Ingredients:

- 1 (12 inch) prepared pizza crust
- ¼ teaspoon Italian seasoning
- ¼ teaspoon crushed red pepper flakes
- 1 cup crumbled goat cheese
- 1 (14 ounce) can quartered artichoke hearts
- 3 plum tomatoes, sliced into ¼-inch thick size
- 6 kalamata olives, pitted and sliced
- ¼ cup fresh basil leaves

Directions:

1. Preheat the oven to 450 degrees F. Grease a baking sheet.
2. Sprinkle the pizza crust with Italian seasoning and red pepper flakes evenly.
3. Place the goat cheese over the crust evenly, leaving about a half-inch of the sides.
4. With the back of a spoon, gently press the cheese downward.
5. Place the artichoke, tomato and olives on top of the cheese.
6. Arrange the pizza crust onto the prepared baking sheet.
7. Bake for about ten to twelve minutes or till the cheese becomes bubbly.
8. Remove from oven and top with the basil.
9. Cut into equal sized wedges and serve.

Nutritional Information per Serving:

Calories	Fat	Carbohydrates	Protein
381	16.1 g	42.4 g	19.4 g

Shrimp Pizza

Yield	Preparation Time	Cooking Time
6 servings	20 minutes	10 minutes

- 1 (12 inch) prepared pizza crust
- 1/3 cup prepared pesto sauce
- 2 cups shredded and divided mozzarella cheese
- 8 ounces cooked shrimp, peeled and deveined
- ½ cup chopped finely sun-dried tomatoes
- ¼ cup minced scallions
- ¼ teaspoon crushed red pepper flakes

Directions:

1. Preheat the oven to 450 degrees F.
2. Arrange the pizza crust onto a baking sheet.
3. Spread the pesto sauce over the crust evenly and sprinkle with half of the cheese.
4. Top with the shrimp, followed by the tomatoes, remaining cheese, scallions, and red pepper flakes.
5. Bake for about ten minutes.
6. Remove from the oven and set aside for about three to five minutes before slicing. Serve

Calories	Fat	Carbohydrates	Protein
202	12.5 g	8.7 g	13.6 g

Pasta with Tomatoes

Yield	Preparation Time	Cooking Time
4 servings	15 minutes	15 minutes

- 8 ounces angel hair pasta
- 2 tablespoons olive oil
- 1 tablespoon minced garlic
- 1 tablespoon crushed dried oregano
- 1 tablespoon crushed dried basil
- 1 teaspoon crushed dried thyme
- 2 cups halved cherry tomatoes

Directions:
1. In a large pan of lightly salted boiling water, add the pasta and cook for about eight to ten minutes or according to the package's directions.
2. Drain the pasta well.
3. In a large skillet, heat the oil over medium heat and sauté the garlic for about one minute.
4. Stir in herbs and sauté for about one minute more.
5. Add the pasta and cook for about two to three minutes or until heated completely.
6. Fold in tomatoes and remove from heat. Serve hot.

Calories	Fat	Carbohydrates	Protein
301	8.9 g	47.7 g	8.5 g

Pasta with Veggies

Yield	Preparation Time	Cooking Time
6 servings	15 minutes	20 minutes

Ingredients:

- 3 tomatoes
- 1 pound pasta
- ¼ cup olive oil
- 1 pound fresh mushrooms, sliced
- 3 garlic cloves, minced
- 1 teaspoon crushed dried oregano
- 1 (2 ounce) can black olives, drained
- ¾ cup crumbled feta cheese

Directions:

1. In a large pan of the salted boiling water, add the tomatoes and cook for about one minute.
2. With a slotted spoon, transfer the tomatoes into a bowl of ice water.
3. In the same pan of the boiling water, add the pasta and cook for about eight to ten minutes.
4. Drain the pasta well.
5. Meanwhile, peel the blanched tomatoes and then chop them.
6. In a large skillet, heat the oil over medium heat and sauté the mushrooms and garlic for about four to five minutes.
7. Add the tomatoes and oregano and cook for about three to four minutes.
8. Divide the pasta onto serving plates and top with the mushroom mixture.
9. Garnish with olives and feta and serve.

Nutritional Information per Serving:

Calories	Fat	Carbohydrates	Protein
446	15.1 g	62.2 g	15.1 g

Pasta with Shrimp & Spinach

Yield	Preparation Time	Cooking Time
4 servings	15 minutes	10 minutes

- 1 cup sour cream
- ½ cup crumbled feta cheese
- 3 garlic cloves, chopped
- 2 teaspoons crushed dried basil
- ¼ teaspoon crushed red pepper flakes
- 8 ounces pasta
- 1 (10 ounce) package frozen spinach, thawed
- 12 ounces medium shrimp, peeled and deveined
- Salt and ground black pepper, as required

Directions:
1. In a large serving bowl, add the sour cream, feta, garlic, basil, red pepper flakes, and salt and mix well.
2. Set aside until using.
3. In a large pan of the lightly salted boiling water, add the fettucine and cook for about ten minutes or according to the package's directions.
4. After eight minutes, stir in the spinach and shrimp and cook for about two minutes.
5. Drain the pasta mixture well.
6. Add the hot pasta mixture into the bowl of the sour cream mixture and gently, toss to coat.
7. Serve immediately.

Calories	Fat	Carbohydrates	Protein
457	19.1 g	38.9 g	32.5 g

Vegetarian Recipes

Roasted Carrots

Yield	Preparation Time	Cooking Time
6 servings	15 minutes	40 minutes

Ingredients:
- 2 pounds carrots, peeled and cut into ½-inch thick slices diagonally
- 2 tablespoons extra-virgin olive oil
- ½ teaspoons red chili powder
- ½ teaspoon ground cinnamon
- Salt and ground black pepper, as required

Directions:
1. Preheat the oven to 400 degrees F. Line a large rimmed baking sheet with parchment paper.
2. In a bowl, add all of the ingredients and toss to coat well.
3. Arrange the carrots onto the prepared baking sheet in a single layer.
4. Roast for about thirty-five to forty minutes, tossing once halfway through.
5. Serve warm.

Nutritional Information per Serving:

Calories	Fat	Carbohydrates	Protein
103	4.7 g	15.1 g	1.3 g

Chickpeas Hummus

Yield	Preparation Time	Cooking Time
4 servings	10 minutes	0

- 1 (15 ounce) can chickpeas, rinsed and drained
- 3 garlic cloves, minced
- ½ teaspoon grated fresh lemon zest
- 1/3 cup olive oil
- 3 tablespoons fresh lemon juice
- 3 tablespoons tahini
- 2 tablespoons plain yogurt
- 1 teaspoon ground cumin
- ¼ teaspoon cayenne pepper
- Salt, as required
- 2 tablespoons chopped fresh parsley

Directions:
1. In a food processor, add all of the ingredients except the pine nuts and pulse until smooth.
2. Transfer the hummus into a serving bowl and refrigerate covered for about one to two hours. Serve with the topping of the parsley.

Calories	Fat	Carbohydrates	Protein
340	24.1 g	22.8 g	8.9 g

Quinoa & Zucchini Fritters

Yield	Preparation Time	Cooking Time
4 servings	20 minutes	18 minutes

Ingredients:

- 1 cup water
- ½ cup quinoa
- 2 cups grated zucchini
- Salt, as required
- 1 cup panko breadcrumbs
- 1 cup grated Parmigiano-Reggiano cheese
- 1 egg
- 3 garlic cloves, minced
- ½ teaspoon dried oregano
- Ground black pepper, as required
- 3 tablespoons olive oil

Directions:

1. In a small pan, add the water and quinoa over medium-high heat and bring to a boil.
2. Reduce the heat to low and simmer covered for about ten minutes.
3. Remove from the heat and, with a fork, fluff the quinoa.
4. Set aside for about ten minutes.
5. Meanwhile, in a colander, place the zucchini and half a teaspoon of salt and toss to coat.
6. Arrange the colander over a sink for at least ten minutes.
7. With paper towels, pat dry the zucchini.
8. In a large bowl, add the zucchini, quinoa, breadcrumbs, cheese, egg, garlic, oregano, salt, and black pepper and mix until well combined.
9. Make 2½-inch patties from the mixture and, with your hands, flatten each slightly.
10. In a large skillet, heat the oil over medium heat and cook the patties in two batches for about four minutes per side or until golden brown.
11. Transfer the fritters onto a paper towel-lined plate to drain.
12. Serve warm.

Nutritional Information per Serving:

Calories	Fat	Carbohydrates	Protein
110	15.8 g	10.3 g	4.8 g

Chickpeas Stew

Yield	Preparation Time	Cooking Time
3 servings	15 minutes	35 minutes

Ingredients:

- 1 tablespoon extra-virgin olive oil
- 1 red bell pepper, seeded and julienned
- 3 scallions, sliced thinly
- 1 jalapeño pepper, chopped
- 2 garlic cloves, minced
- ½ teaspoon ground cumin
- ½ teaspoon paprika
- 1 (28 ounce) can whole, peeled tomatoes, crushed
- Pinch of brown sugar
- Salt and ground black pepper, as required
- ½ cup vegetable broth
- 2 cups canned chickpeas
- 2 tablespoons minced fresh parsley
- 1 teaspoon grated fresh lemon zest

Directions:

1. In a pan, heat the oil over medium heat and sauté the bell pepper, scallions, jalapeño, garlic, cumin, and paprika for about four to five minutes.
2. Stir in the tomatoes, brown sugar, salt, black pepper, and broth and simmer for about twenty minutes.
3. Stir in the chickpeas, parsley, and lemon zest and simmer for about ten minutes.
4. Serve hot.

Nutritional Information per Serving:

Calories	Fat	Carbohydrates	Protein
280	7.1 g	41.6 g	14.9 g

Stuffed Tomatoes

Yield	Preparation Time	Cooking Time
2 servings	15 minutes	5 minutes

- 2 large tomatoes, halved crosswise
- ¼ cup pitted and sliced Kalamata olives
- 2 tablespoons chopped fresh basil
- ¼ cup crumbled feta cheese
- ½ cup garlic croutons
- 2 tablespoons balsamic vinaigrette

Directions:
1. Preheat the broiler of the oven. Arrange the oven rack about four to five inches from the heating element.
2. With your fingers, remove the seeds from the tomato halves.
3. Carefully run a small knife around the pulp vertically, not touching the bottom and then, gently remove the pulp.
4. Chop the tomato pulp and transfer into a bowl.
5. Arrange the tomatoes over the paper towels, cut side down to drain.
6. In the bowl of tomato pulp, add the remaining ingredients and mix well.
7. Stuff the tomatoes with olive mixture evenly.
8. Arrange the tomatoes onto a broiler pan and broil for about five minutes or until cheese is melted. Serve warm.

Calories	Fat	Carbohydrates	Protein
193	12.7 g	15.5 g	5.4 g

Dessert Recipes

Roasted Pears

Yield	Preparation Time	Cooking Time
6 servings	15 minutes	25 minutes

Ingredients:

- ¼ cup pear nectar
- 3 tablespoons honey
- 2 tablespoons butter, melted
- 1 teaspoon grated fresh orange zest
- 3 ripe medium Bosc pears, peeled and cored
- ½ cup mascarpone cheese
- 2 tablespoons powdered sugar
- 1/3 cup chopped walnuts

Directions:

1. Preheat the oven to 400 degrees F.
2. In a bowl, add the pear nectar, honey, butter, and orange zest and mix well.
3. In a two-quart rectangular baking dish, arrange the pears, cut sides down, and top with the honey mixture.

4. Roast for about twenty to twenty-five minutes, spooning liquid over the pears occasionally.
5. Remove from the oven and transfer the pears onto serving plates with some of the cooking liquid.
6. In a bowl, add the mascarpone cheese and powdered sugar and mix well.
7. Top the pears with the cheese mixture and serve with the garnishing of walnuts.

Nutritional Information per Serving:

Calories	Fat	Carbohydrates	Protein
222	10.8 g	30.3 g	4.5 g

Chocolate Mousse

Yield	Preparation Time	Cooking Time
4 servings	15 minutes	5 minutes

- 3 ½ ounces dark chocolate, chopped
- ¾ cup milk
- 1 tablespoon honey
- ½ teaspoon vanilla extract
- 2 cups plain Greek yogurt
- 2 tablespoons fresh raspberries

Directions:
1. In a pan, add the chocolate and milk over medium-low heat and cook for about three to five minutes or until the chocolate melts, stirring continuously.
2. Add the honey and vanilla extract and stir to combine well.
3. Remove from the heat and set aside at room temperature to cool slightly.
4. In a large glass bowl, place the yogurt and chocolate mixture and gently, stir to combine.
5. Refrigerate to chill for about two hours.
6. Serve with the topping of raspberries.

Calories	Fat	Carbohydrates	Protein
262	9.8 g	30.5 g	10.5 g

Frozen Strawberry Yogurt

Yield	Preparation Time	Cooking Time
6 servings	15 minutes	0

Ingredients:
- 4 cups frozen strawberries
- ½ cup plain Greek yogurt
- 3 tablespoons honey
- 2 teaspoons pure vanilla extract
- Pinch of salt
- 1 tablespoon fresh mint leaves

Directions:
1. In a food processor, add all of the ingredients except the mint and pulse until smooth.
2. Serve immediately with the garnishing of mint leaves.

Nutritional Information per Serving:

Calories	Fat	Carbohydrates	Protein
126	0.4 g	28.5 g	1.8 g

Tahini Cookies

Yield	Preparation Time	Cooking Time
30 servings	20 minutes	15 minutes

Ingredients:

- 1 ½ cups whole-wheat pastry flour
- 1 tablespoon baking soda
- Pinch of salt
- ¾ cup sugar
- ½ cup butter, softened
- ½ cup tahini
- 1 tablespoon orange blossom water
- 1 tablespoon honey
- 1 medium egg

Directions:

1. In a large bowl, mix together the flour, baking soda, and salt.
2. In the bowl of a stand mixer, add the sugar and butter and beat on medium-high speed until light and fluffy.
3. Add the tahini and beat well.
4. Add the orange blossom water and honey and beat until well combined.
5. Add the egg and beat on low speed until well combined.
6. Slowly add the flour mixture, mixing well until a dough forms.
7. With plastic wrap, cover the bowl and refrigerate for about one hour.
8. Preheat the oven to 350 degrees F. Line two baking sheets with parchment paper.
9. With two tablespoons of dough, make balls and arrange onto the prepared baking sheets about three inches apart.
10. With the back of a lightly floured fork, gently flatten each ball.
11. Bake for about thirteen to fifteen minutes or until golden brown.
12. Remove from the oven and place the baking sheets onto the wire racks for about five minutes.
13. Carefully invert the cookies onto the wire racks to cool completely before serving.

Nutritional Information per Serving:

Calories	Fat	Carbohydrates	Protein
97	5.4 g	11.2 g	1.5 g

Baklava

Yield	Preparation Time	Cooking Time
18 servings	20 minutes	50 minutes

Ingredients:

- 1 pound nuts (pistachios, almonds, walnuts), chopped
- 1 teaspoon ground cinnamon
- 1 (16 ounce) package phyllo dough
- 1 cup butter, melted
- 1 cup white sugar
- 1 cup water
- ½ cup honey
- 1 teaspoon vanilla extract

Directions:

1. Preheat the oven to 350 degrees F. Grease a 9x13-inch baking dish.
2. In a bowl, add the nuts and cinnamon and toss to coat well.
3. Set aside.
4. Unroll the phyllo dough and cut in half.
5. Arrange two dough sheets into the prepared baking dish and coat with some butter.
6. Repeat with eight dough sheets in layers and sprinkle with 2-3 tablespoons of nut mixture.
7. Repeat with remaining dough sheets, butter and nuts.
8. With a sharp knife, cut into diamond shapes all the way to the bottom of the baking dish.
9. Bake for about 50 minutes or until top becomes golden and crisp.
10. Meanwhile, for the sauce: in a pan, add the sugar and water and cook until the sugar is melted, stirring continuously.
11. Stir in the honey and vanilla extract and simmer for about twenty minutes.
12. Remove the baklava from oven and immediately place the sauce on top evenly.
13. Set aside to cool before serving.

Nutritional Information per Serving:

Calories	Fat	Carbohydrates	Protein
435	27.8 g	43.5 g	7.1 g

Can I ask you for a Quick Favor?

Would you, please, leave this book review on Amazon?

Reviews are very important for me as they help me to sell more books and to understand how to move forward. This will enable me to write more books.

Thank you for reading so much!

Want more?

Visit my site for bonuses:

Meal plan + Shopping list

https://ellenbranson.wixsite.com/mysite

I am sure you will love it!

Thank you!

Ellen Branson

Other books by Ellen:

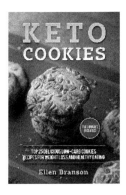

Made in the USA
Middletown, DE
22 April 2019